The Blue Peter Book of
Gorgeous Grub

The Blue Peter Book of

Gorgeous Grub

edited by
Biddy Baxter

illustrated by
Anni Axeworthy

Home Economist: Elaine Bastable

photographs by David Clark

A Piccolo Original
Piccolo Books in association with
the British Broadcasting Corporation

This book is dedicated to
the 33,250 'Blue Peter' viewers who
sent us their favourite recipes

First published 1980 by Pan Books Ltd,
Cavaye Place, London SW10 9PG in association with
the British Broadcasting Corporation
35 Marylebone High Street, London W1
This collection © the British Broadcasting Corporation
1980
recipes © the contributors 1980
illustrations © Anni Axeworthy 1980
PAN ISBN 0 330 26195 9
BBC ISBN 0 563 17844 2
Printed in Great Britain by
C. Nicholls & Company Ltd,
Philips Park Press, Manchester

Contents

Main Meals

Hot and Cold Puddings

Sweets and Drinks

Introduction

Do *you* like the sound of Pigs in Blankets, Stinging Nettle Spinach, Eggomanics Toadstools or Bat Pie?

They were four of the more unusual of the 33,250 entries we received for our Gorgeous Grub competition. They didn't win a prize, but they were certainly out of the ordinary and quite a change from the hundreds of suggestions people sent in for custard and sausage and chips and roast dinners.

The idea was for Blue Peter viewers to give us their *favourite* recipes. Not something they'd invented, but dishes they'd tried and tasted and thoroughly enjoyed – a sort of cookery Top of the Pops contest, and we were all intrigued and surprised by the suggestions that came pouring in.

First of all, it seems that Blue Peter viewers from all over Britain are very keen on food! We had entries from places as far apart as the Isle of Lewis and the Channel Islands to Lowestoft and Anglesey.

After talking to all the people in the Blue Peter office, we'd come to the conclusion that savouries would be more popular than sweets. But how wrong we were! After sifting through all the Gorgeous Grub entries, we discovered that recipes for sweet things outnumbered the savouries by at least four to one.

Out of the savouries, corned beef and sausage meat were two of the favourite ingredients, with cheese and baked potatoes hard on their heels.

Out of the suggestions for puddings and sweets, chocolate proved to be by far the most popular ingredient and we had hundreds of recipes for chocolate crunches, which all sounded delicious, but we didn't fancy the idea of a mixture of instant mashed potato and drinking chocolate that someone sent in. Other top recipes were for brownies, flapjacks, gingerbread and biscuits and that delicious pud the Pavlova cake.

Viewers' favourite fruits were banana, pineapple and raspberry, and several people sent in recipes that were a mixture of sweet and savoury ingredients – like Fish Finger and Banana Delight.

One useful thing we discovered from this competition was a foolproof way of slimming – you've no idea how poring over hundreds of recipes puts you off food! We used to come into the Blue Peter office where the recipes were being sorted whenever we weren't in the studio or filming and we soon found out that after two or three hours of reading Gorgeous Grub entries, we didn't feel like eating a thing.

One day, the final straw was coming across Neil's Supper Sandwich, a mixture of Marmite, cucumber, cottage cheese and strawberry jam topped with a fried egg!

Other unusual ideas were Limited Omelette, described as 'for anyone who, for various reasons, has limited food', Peruvian Chocolate Potato Cake from a viewer who used to live in Peru, Denis Healey – a dish looking like a face with sausage eyebrows – Hippo Hot Pot, Egg Men and Dad's Skirley which is the Boath family's favourite holiday meal 'called after Dad because he is the only one who can make it – Mum always burns it'.

As always, we tried very hard to be absolutely fair with the judging. In the end, the only way to decide who wins a competition like this is by thinking of your own likes and dislikes and by taking into consideration the originality of the recipes. But we were very lucky to have top cook Delia Smith as our chief judge, and it was Delia who selected the final forty first-prize winning ideas.

The two main things Delia looked for were no expensive ingredients and no complicated cooking methods, and after we'd announced the results on Blue Peter, Delia demonstrated one of the top forty dishes, Mrs Wilkinson's Parsley Scone, which you'll find on page 15. Apart from tasting good, this particular recipe is quick and easy as well as being economical and with the addition of parsley, fresh from the Blue Peter garden, we all gave it top marks!

We hope you enjoy trying out *all* the Top Forty recipes, and we'd like to say thank you to the people who helped behind-the-scenes to make the competition and the book possible. Our friends Hazel Gill, Sandra Swetman, Christine Beynon and Rosemary Evans had the mammoth task of opening all the entries and sorting them into sections so that we could make up the shortlist for Delia. And Elaine Bastable and Kim Richards followed that with a colossal cook-in to make sure each of the potential prize-winning suggestions really *did* work.

The nice thing is that this has ended up a double purpose book. It's not only a very good guide to producing mouth-watering meals and snacks, it's also helping children in need all over the world. Fifty per cent of the proceeds of each copy of *Gorgeous Grub* is being donated to the International Year of the Child, and even the forty dishes we displayed in the studio helped a good cause. We auctioned them off to the camera crew, the studio engineers and the scene crew after the programme, and raised nearly £25 for our Great Blue Peter Bring & Buy Sale Appeal!

Simon Groom.

Chris Wenner

Tina Heath x

PS   If we'd awarded a prize for the shortest entry, it would have gone to the viewer who simply said 'I like chips'!

Notes

Some of the contributors sent in their recipes giving the quantities in ounces and some in grammes. We have, therefore, printed the recipes giving *both* measurements so that you can use whichever you prefer – *remembering not to mix the two.*

You should find all the equipment and utensils that you need to cook these recipes in your own kitchen, but check with a grown up before you begin.

Safety in the kitchen

If you are just learning to cook, make sure that a grown up or elder brother or sister is around to give you a hand.

Please remember

1   That knives are sharp – be careful

2   To keep pan handles turned towards the back of the cooker

3   To turn the oven off when your baking is done

4   To wipe up any spills immediately

5   To wash your hands before you start

6   Always use an oven glove or a thick dry cloth to take things from the oven

Cookery terms

Preparation

COMBINING: mixing ingredients thoroughly together, with a spoon or clean hands

BEATING: mixing ingredients briskly to blend them together. A wooden spoon is usually best for this

CREAMING: mixing two ingredients together until they are soft and fluffy. A wooden spoon makes this easy

FOLDING: cutting, lifting and turning a mixture gently to lightly blend ingredients together. A metal spoon is the right utensil for this.

RUBBING IN: mixing fat ingredients using your fingertips, to give a crumbly mixture

WHISKING: a hand whisk or rotary whisk is used briskly to beat air into cream or egg whites to make them stiff

Cooking

BAKING: cooking food in the oven, like Sandie's Raisin Bread

BOILING: cooking food in liquid at boiling point (212°F, 100°C), like Cabbage Parcels

FRYING: cooking food in fat, like Curried Potato Cakes

GRILLING: cooking under the grill in a quick heat, like Butterscotch Bananas

SIMMERING: steady, slow cooking in liquid on low heat, like Onion and Potato Soup

Savoury Snacks

Mrs Wilkinson's
Parsley Scone

Ingredients

2 ounces (50 grammes) bacon
8 ounces (225 grammes) self-raising flour
½ teaspoon (½ x 5 millilitre spoon) salt
1 ounce (25 grammes) butter
4 ounces (100 grammes) cheese
¼ pint (150 millilitres) milk
1 tablespoon (1 × 15 millilitre spoon) tomato
    ketchup, dash of worcester sauce
1 tablespoon (1 × 15 millilitre spoon) freshly
    chopped parsley
    milk to glaze

Method

Remove the rind from the bacon. Grill or fry until crisp and cut into pieces.

Sieve together the flour and the salt, and rub in the butter.

Add 3 ounces (75 grammes) of the cheese, all the chopped bacon and all the chopped parsley.

Mix together the milk, tomato ketchup and worcester sauce, and add to the dry ingredients.

Mix to a soft dough and roll out on a floured surface to a 7 inch (18 centimetre) round.

Brush with the milk, sprinkle with the remaining cheese and mark into wedges.

Place on a greased baking sheet.

Bake at 400 °F, 200 °C, gas mark 6, for 30 minutes.

Makes 8

DIANE GLENN
Age 14
Sheffield, South Yorkshire

Potato and Onion Soup

Ingredients

1 ounce (25 grammes) butter
1 pound (450 grammes) potatoes
1 medium onion (4 ounces; 100 grammes)
1 pint (575 millilitres) water
1 beef or ham stock cube
salt and black pepper
4 tablespoons (4 × 15 millilitre spoons) top of
   the milk *or* single cream
1 tablespoon (1 × 15 millilitre spoon) parsley
   (fresh or dried) – optional

Method

Skin the onion and peel the potatoes.

Thinly slice the potatoes and the onion.

Melt the butter in a saucepan, add the potatoes and
the onion and cook gently *without browning*, with the lid
on the pan, for 10 minutes until the potatoes are soft.

Add the water and the stock cube.

Bring to the boil and simmer gently for about 15
minutes.

Now sieve or liquidize the soup.

Wash and chop parsley if fresh.

Add the milk, or cream, to the soup and bring back to the boil.

Add the parsley.

Taste and correct the seasoning.

VARIATION
1 ounce of grated cheese can be sprinkled on the soup in place of the parsley.

Serves 3

CAROLINE SMITH
Age 14
Glenrothes, Fife

Quick Bacon Savoury Rice

Ingredients

3 ounces (75 grammes) butter
6 ounces (175 grammes; about 6 rashers) bacon
4 ounces (100 grammes) mushrooms
8 ounces (225 grammes) long grain rice
1 small onion (2 ounces; 50 grammes)
salt and pepper
watercress for a garnish

Method

Cook the rice in boiling salted water for 15 minutes.

Drain.

Remove rinds from bacon and cut into small pieces.

Wash and slice mushrooms.

Peel and finely chop onion.

Melt 2 ounces (50 grammes) of the butter in a large pan. Fry the onion for 10 minutes, until soft and golden.

Add the bacon and fry for 4 minutes.

Add the remaining 1 ounce (25 grammes) butter and the mushrooms and cook, stirring, for about another 4 minutes.

Stir in the cooked rice and plenty of salt and pepper.

Heat through until piping hot.

Put the mixture on to a serving dish and garnish with watercress.

I am sure you will find this savoury recipe very appetizing.

Serves 3–4

Janet Dornan
Age 13
Belfast

Courgette à la Greque

This recipe can be very useful for vegetarians as well as other people.

Ingredients

1 pound (450 grammes) small courgettes
1 clove garlic, crushed
1 small onion (2 ounces; 50 grammes)
1 level teaspoon (1 × 5 millilitre spoon) dried basil
¼ pound (100 grammes) tiny button mushrooms
salt and pepper
1 ounce (25 grammes) butter
small tin (8 ounces; 225 grammes) tomatoes

Method

First fry chopped onion and crushed garlic in the butter for about 5 minutes, keeping the lid on the pan. Then add the mushrooms, leaving them whole.

Add courgettes, replace the lid and simmer gently for about 10 minutes until soft. The courgettes must be cut into ½ inch (1 centimetre) slices with the skin on – like a cucumber – before adding.

Add the tomatoes, the basil and seasoning. Leave on low heat with the lid on, stirring now and again for about 20 minutes.

Cheese can be grated on when serving with mashed potatoes and greens.

Serves 4

RACHAEL RAWNSLEY
Age 13
St Austell, Cornwall

Cheese Strudel

Ingredients

14 ounce (397 grammes) packet frozen pastry
  (thawed)
6 ounces (175 grammes) cheese (preferably
  strong cheddar)
$\frac{1}{4}$ pound (100 grammes) mushrooms, sliced
$\frac{1}{4}$ pound (100 grammes) ham
1 small onion (2 ounces; 50 grammes), chopped
1 ounce (25 grammes) butter
salt and pepper
milk for brushing

Method

Melt the butter in a frying pan. Add the chopped
onion and fry until golden brown.

Add the sliced mushrooms and fry until soft.

Cut the ham into small squares and add to the pan.

Grate or thinly cut the cheese (it doesn't matter which).

Take the pan off the heat, then stir in the cheese.

Season well with salt and pepper.

Roll the pastry thinly to a large square and trim to
about 15 × 15 inches (38 × 38 centimetres).

Cut the pastry in half, lay one half on a baking sheet and brush the edges with milk.

Spread the filling to within $\frac{1}{2}$ inch (1 centimetre) of the edge.

Cover with the other half of the pastry. Seal edges firmly and mark a criss-cross pattern over the top with the back of a knife – don't cut through.

Brush with milk.

Cook at 425 °F, 220 °C, gas mark 7, for about 30 minutes or until golden brown.

Eat hot with bread.

Serves 5–6

HELEN KEENE
Age 13
Sale, Cheshire

Curried Potato Cakes

Our cat really likes them !

Ingredients

1 ounce (2 grammes) butter
1 pound (450 grammes) peeled potatoes (1½ pounds; 675 grammes) with peel on)
2 medium-sized onions (about 4 ounces; 100 grammes)
3 ounces (75 grammes) cheese
salt and pepper
1 ounce (25 grammes) fresh white breadcrumbs ⎫
½ ounce (15 grammes) curry powder ⎬ mixed together
oil for frying

Method

Cook potatoes in boiling salted water. Mash with $\frac{1}{2}$ ounce (15 grammes) of the butter and leave to cool.

Chop onions finely and fry in the remaining $\frac{1}{2}$ ounce (15 grammes) of the butter until golden brown.

Grate cheese.

Mix potatoes, onions and cheese together, and season with salt and pepper.

Divide the mixture into eight pieces and shape into cakes.

Roll cakes in breadcrumbs and curry powder.

Fry for 4–6 minutes on each side in hot shallow oil.

Makes 8

JAMES CHANT, Age 9
LISA CHANT, Age 6
Haslemere, Surrey

Tauli

A filling vegetable dish which can be eaten on its own, or as an accompaniment to sausages, fishfingers or beefburgers.

Ingredients

2 medium onions (8 ounces; 225 grammes), sliced

3 ounces (75 grammes) fat (preferably dripping)

1 pound (450 grammes) skinned fresh tomatoes (cut up) or 1 large tin (14 ounces; 397 grammes) tomatoes

1 pound (450 grammes) peeled carrots, cut into $\frac{1}{2}$ inch (1 centimetre) dice

2 pounds (900 grammes) peeled potatoes, cut into $\frac{1}{2}$ inch (1 centimetre) dice

salt and pepper to taste

Method

Fry the onions in the fat until golden brown (don't let them burn).

Add the tomatoes, carrots and cook for $\frac{1}{2}$ hour with the lid on the pan.

Then add the potatoes and plenty of salt and pepper.

Cook on *low* heat, keeping the lid on, stirring frequently to prevent burning for a further 30–40 minutes until the vegetables are tender.

Cooking time is about $1-1\frac{1}{4}$ hours from the start.

If you like a hot dish, add a little crushed red pepper or any other flavouring you like, e.g. worcester sauce, 10 minutes before serving.

NOTE *any root vegetable can be used to your taste.*

Serves 4

ANDREW WALLACE
Age 8
London

28

Crunchy Sausage Rolls

*They are very tasty for parties or
supper snacks.*

Ingredients

8 slices of thin white bread
4 ounces (100 grammes) red leicester or cheddar
   cheese – grated
2 ounces (50 grammes) butter, softened
salt and pepper
8 pork chipolata sausages
$\frac{1}{2}$ level teaspoon ($\frac{1}{2} \times 5$ millilitre spoon) mustard
16 wooden cocktail sticks

Method

Remove crusts from slices of bread and roll flat with
rolling pin.

Mix butter, grated cheese, salt, pepper and mustard
together.

Spread mixture on
slices of bread.

Place a sausage on
each slice and roll up.

Secure bread with
a cocktail stick at
each end and cut
the rolls in half.

Place on greased baking sheet.

Bake in oven 400 °F, 200 °C, gas mark 6, for 25–30 minutes until crisp.

Serve hot.

Makes 16

DAVID SINGLETON
Age 14
Bradford, West Yorkshire

Cucumber Sweet and Sour

Ingredients

1 large cucumber
salt
1 very small onion (1 ounce; 25 grammes),
   skinned
2 gherkins
1½ ounces (40 grammes) sultanas
5 fluid ounce carton (142 millilitres) soured
   cream
2 tablespoons (2 × 15 millilitre spoons) lemon
   juice
1 level teaspoon (1 × 5 millilitre spoon) castor
   sugar
dash of Tabasco
freshly ground black
   pepper

Method

Peel the cucumber and
slice thinly.

Layer in a dish, sprinkling
salt between the layers.

Leave for 2–3 hours.

Chop the onion, gherkins and sultanas and blend into the soured cream with the lemon juice, sugar, Tabasco, and pepper.

Drain the cucumber, and dry on sheets of absorbent kitchen paper. Fold the cream mixture through the cucumber.

Serve chilled in individual dishes.

Serves 6–8

ROBERT IRELAND
Age 7
Sidcup, Kent

Nasi Goreng

This dish comes from Malaysia and is really delicious.

Ingredients

10 ounces (275 grammes) long grain rice
4 ounces (100 grammes) diced ham
1 medium onion (4 ounces; 100 grammes) chopped
½ teaspoon (½ × 5 millilitre spoon) chilli powder – or a little more to your taste
3 ounces (75 grammes) butter
crushed clove of garlic
1 teaspoon (1 × 5 millilitre spoon) ground coriander
2 eggs
4 ounces (100 grammes) prawns (fresh or frozen)

Method

Cook the rice in boiling salted water for about 15 minutes and drain.

Fry the onions gently for 10 minutes in 2 ounces (50 grammes) of the butter with chilli powder, coriander and garlic, keeping the lid on the pan.

Add the remaining 1 ounce (25 grammes) of the butter, add ham and fry for 2 minutes.

Add the cooked rice and prawns to the pan and keep hot, stirring frequently.

Then make an omelette with the 2 eggs: beat the eggs in a basin with salt and pepper and 1 tablespoon (1 × 15 millilitre spoon) of milk.

Melt ½ ounce (15 grammes) butter in a frying pan.

When the butter is just starting to brown, pour in the eggs. Keeping the heat fairly high, shake the pan and stir a little with a fork. When the underside is brown, fold the omelette in half and cook for another minute.

Dice and lay on top of the rice mixture.

Serve hot.

Serves 3

SAMANTHA HILLS
Age 12
Salisbury, Wiltshire

Cakes and Biscuits

Sesame Snaps

Ingredients

6 ounces (175 grammes) butter or margarine
3 ounces (1 heaped tablespoon; 1 × 15
    millilitre spoon) honey or treacle
4½ ounces (115 grammes) dessicated coconut
3 ounces (75 grammes) brown sugar
2 ounces (50 grammes) sesame seeds
6 ounces (175 grammes) rolled oats

Method

Toast the sesame seeds under the grill for a few minutes.

Melt the butter slowly over a low heat.

Add the brown sugar and honey (or treacle), stirring all the time with a wooden spoon.

Add sesame seeds and keep stirring to blend evenly.

Add coconut and oats, stirring and pressing the mixture together.

Press the mixture into a greased swiss roll tin (13 × 9 inches; 32 × 23 centimetres).

Bake at 300 °F, 150 °C, gas mark 2, for about ½ hour.

Check the baking as honey burns easily.

Mark into 24 squares, while still warm and leave in the tin to get cold. Then cut through.

Makes 24

CHARLOTTE CUMMINGS
Age 13
Cambridge

Sugary Apple Muffins

Ingredients

4 ounces (100 grammes) self-raising flour
2 ounces (50 grammes) margarine
2 ounces (50 grammes) caster sugar
3 ounces (75 grammes) finely chopped apple
1 egg
1 teaspoon (1 × 5 millilitre spoon) baking
   powder
¼ teaspoon (¼ × 5 millilitre spoon) cinnamon
¼ teaspoon (¼ × 5 millilitre spoon) nutmeg
1 tablespoon (1 × 15 millilitre spoon) milk

Method

Cream the margarine
and the sugar together.

Beat in the egg.

Mix the flour, baking
powder and spices
and fold in with the
milk to the creamed
mixture.

Fold in apple and fill 12 baking cases with the mixture.

Sprinkle an extra tablespoon (1 × 15 millilitre spoon) sugar mixed with spices over the tops if liked.

Bake at 425 °F, 220 °C, gas mark 7, for 15 minutes.

Makes 12

LORRAINE ANDERSON
Age 15
Alton, Hants.

Goosnargh Cakes

Ingredients

9 ounces (255 grammes) plain flour
pinch of salt
2 level teaspoons (2 × 5 millilitre spoons)
    coriander powder
½ teaspoon (½ × 5 millilitre spoon) carraway
    seeds
6 ounces (175 grammes) butter (fresh farm butter
    makes the best Goosnargh cakes
2 ounces (50 grammes) caster sugar to coat

NOTE *the coriander powder and carraway seeds give
the Goosnargh Cakes a delicate flavour.*

Method

Mix together flour, salt, coriander powder and
carraway seeds.

Rub in the butter, then knead to a smooth dough with
hands.

Roll out on a floured board until about a quarter inch
(½ centimetre) thick.

Cut into 2 inch (5 centimetre) rounds with a plain
cutter – a wineglass would do.

Place on a greased baking sheet and coat liberally with
caster sugar.

Bake in a slow oven, 250 °F, 120 °C, or gas mark ½, for 30 minutes until firm but not golden. They should be pale in colour.

While still warm, sift on more sugar.

When cool, put in a tin.

Makes 24

ELIZABETH DAINTY
Age 11
Bayhouse, Lancaster

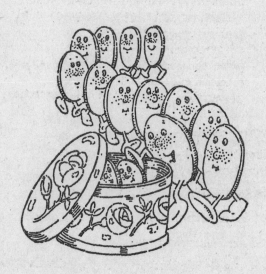

Marmalade Cake

Ingredients

8 ounces (225 grammes) plain flour
pinch of salt
3 level teaspoons (3 × 5 millilitre spoons) baking
   powder
4 ounces (100 grammes) butter
2 ounces (50 grammes) caster sugar
1 level teaspoon (1 × 5 millilitre spoon) finely
   grated orange rind
2 eggs, beaten
3 level tablespoons (3 × 15 millilitre spoons)
   thick orange marmalade
2 level tablespoons (2 × 15 millilitre spoons) milk

Method

Line a 7 inch (18 centimetre) round cake tin with greased greaseproof paper.

Sift flour, salt and baking powder into bowl.

Rub in the butter finely.

Add sugar and orange rind.

Beat to fairly soft mixture with eggs, marmalade and milk.

Transfer to prepared tin. Bake in centre of moderate oven, 350 °F, 180 °C, gas mark 4, for 1–1¼ hours (or until

a wooden cocktail stick inserted into centre comes out clean).

Leave in tin for 5 minutes. Turn out on to wire cooling rack.

Peel off paper. Store cake in airtight tin when cold.

Makes 6–8 portions

COLLETE SHARKEY
Age 12
Wigan, Lancashire

Cashew Nut Biscuits

This recipe was sent to my mum by a Quaker. They are really scrumptious biscuits. I make about 15 and they are gone within the night !

Ingredients

8 ounces (225 grammes) wholemeal flour
4 ounces (100 grammes) ground cashew nuts
6 ounces (175 grammes) soft brown sugar
1 egg, beaten with one tablespoon (1 × 15 millilitre spoon) milk
3 ounces (75 grammes) butter or margarine
1 ounce (25 grammes) whole cashew nuts – optional

Method

Rub fat into flour, nuts and sugar.

Mix to a firm dough with beaten egg and milk.

Roll out on floured board. Roll to $\frac{1}{8}$ inch ($\frac{1}{2}$ centimetre) thick and cut with a 3 inch (7 centimetre) pastry cutter into rounds.

Decorate with whole cashew nuts if you like.

Bake for 15–20 minutes at 350 °F, 180 °C, gas mark 4.

Let them cool for 15 minutes, then they are ready to eat.

NOTE *if you haven't got a nut mill, the health food shops will grind them for you.*

Makes about 20

DEBORAH HOBSON
Age 11
Scunthorpe, South Humberside

Banana, Date and Honey Cake

Ingredients

5 ounces (125 grammes) wholemeal flour
5 ounces (125 grammes) white self-raising flour
1 teaspoon (1 × 5 millilitre spoon) baking powder
pinch of salt
5 ounces (125 grammes) margarine
1 egg
5 ounces (125 grammes) ripe mashed banana
   (skinned)
6 ounces (175 grammes) chopped dates
2 tablespoons (2 × 15 millilitre spoons) runny
   honey
4 ounces (100 grammes) soft brown sugar

Method

Cream margarine and
sugar together.

Beat in egg.

Add mashed banana and
honey and beat well.

Stir in chopped dates.

Mix flour, baking powder, and salt together and stir into creamed mixture.

When well mixed, turn into a greased oblong tin (9 × 5 × 3 inches; 23 × 13 × 7 centimetres) or a round cake tin (7 inches; 18 centimetres).

Bake on centre shelf of the oven, at 325 °F, 170 °C, gas mark 3, for about $1\frac{1}{4}$ hours, or until centre of cake feels firm.

Makes 8–10 slices

MARIE ROLLASON
Age 9
London

Oatmeal Cookies

Ingredients

3 ounces (75 grammes) plain flour
4 ounces (100 grammes) rolled oats
2 ounces (50 grammes) caster sugar
4 ounces (100 grammes) margarine
1 level tablespoon (1 × 15 millilitre spoon)
   golden syrup
½ level teaspoon (½ × 5 millilitre spoon)
   bicarbonate soda
2 teaspoons (2 × 5 millilitre spoons) boiling
   water

Method

Preheat oven to 350 °F, 180 °C, gas mark 4.

Mix the flour, oats and sugar in a basin.

Over a low heat, melt the margarine and golden syrup in a medium sized saucepan.

Dissolve the bicarbonate of soda in the boiling water, which will bubble. Add this to the margarine and syrup.

Pour on to the dry ingredients and mix well with a wooden spoon.

On the day we announced the Competition results on the programme Delia held a 'Cook-In' and demonstrated Mrs Wilkinson's Parsley Scone using parsley freshly picked from the Blue Peter garden. We all enjoyed having a taste – and spreading the slices with butter gave the scone that extra touch of luxury!

Savoury Snacks

Mrs Wilkinson's Parsley Scone

Potato and Onion Soup

Quick Bacon Savoury Rice

Courgette à la Grecque

Cheese Strudel

Curried Potato Cakes

Tauli

Crunchy Sausage Rolls

Cucumber Sweet and Sour

Nasi Goreng

Cakes and Biscuits

Sesame Snaps

Sugary Apple Muffins

Goosnargh Cakes

Marmalade Cake

Cashew Nut Biscuits

Banana, Date and
Honey Cake

Oatmeal Cookies

Crunchy Chocolate
Cookies

Sandie's Raisin Bread

Peanut Bars

'Star Wars' Stew

Main Meals

Eggs Essen

Orkney Bacon Savoury

Sausage Lasagne

Cabbage Parcels

Orange Chicken with
Rosemary

Chicken Yoghurt

Guinness Hot Pot

Kipper and Egg Flan

Hot and Cold Puddings

Granny's Lemon Pudding

No-Bake Banana Cheesecake

Butterscotch Bananas

Cranachan

Apple and Honey Dessert

Bramble Bombe

Sweets and Drinks

Honey Health Candy

Grandma's Stick Jaw Toffee

Mocha Fudge

Orange Cocktail

Strawberry Marshmallow Float Drink

With wet hands, roll mixture into 20–24 small balls and place them well apart on a greased baking tray. Bake in the centre of the oven for 10–12 minutes or until golden brown.

Leave to cool on the baking tray for 3 minutes, then transfer to a cooling rack.

For extra special cookies: like nut cookies, add 1 ounce (25 grammes) chopped nuts; for cherry cookies, add 1 ounce (25 grammes) chopped glacé cherries; for raisin cookies, add 1 ounce (25 grammes) raisins.

Happy eating !

Makes about 20

LISA KING
Age 15
Newmarket, Suffolk

Crunchy Chocolate Cookies

Ingredients

4 ounces (100 grammes) soft-blend margarine
4 ounces (100 grammes) plain flour
1 tablespoon (1 × 15 millilitre spoon) cocoa
2 ounces (50 grammes) soft brown sugar
½ ounce (15 grammes) crushed bran flakes
12 jellytots or glacé cherry pieces – optional
Preheat oven at 350 °F, 180 °C, gas mark 4

Method

Sieve the flour, and cocoa into a mixing bowl. Add the sugar and margarine and stir to form a stiff dough.

Using a little flour, bring together using fingertips.

On a lightly floured table, roll mixture into a sausage and divide into 12 pieces.

Shape each piece into a ball, roll in crushed bran flakes flatten slightly, and place each 2 inches (5 centimetres) apart on a greased baking tray.

Place sweet or cherry if you have them, in centre.

Bake just above centre of oven for about 15 minutes until they are slightly cracked and flatter.

Cool on a wire tray.

I have made these,
they are delicious.

Makes 12

TIMOTHY JAMES
Age 10
Castletown, Isle of Man

Sandie's Raisin Bread:
for eating with honey

Ingredients

12 ounces (350 grammes) self-raising flour
large pinch of salt
3 ounces (75 grammes) caster sugar
1½ ounces (40 grammes) broken walnuts
3 ounces (75 grammes) seedless raisins (or mixed
   fruit)
2 eggs
7 fluid ounces (200 millilitres) milk
2 ounces (50 grammes) butter

THE GLAZE
1 tablespoon (1 × 15 millilitre spoon) castor
   sugar
2 tablespoons (2 × 15 millilitre spoons) milk

Method

You will need a large bowl, a sieve and a wooden spoon
for mixing the bread, a small bowl for mixing the eggs
and a small saucepan for melting the butter and making
the glaze. You will also need a sharp knife and a pastry
brush. Also a loaf tin about 9 × 5 × 3 inches
(23 × 13 × 7 centimetres) and grease it lightly. Turn
on oven to moderate – 350 °F, 180 °C, gas mark 4, and
find a pair of oven gloves.

Sift the flour and salt together into a large bowl and
add the sugar.

Cut up the walnuts coarsely using the knife and add to the flour, together with the raisins (or mixed fruit).

Stir well and hollow out the centre of the mixture.

Melt the butter in a saucepan over low heat.

Lightly beat the eggs. Pour eggs into the centre of the flour mixture and add the milk. Using a wooden spoon, mix to a soft dough.

Stir in the melted butter and mix thoroughly.

Pour into the greased loaf tin and spread evenly.

Place in the centre of the preheated oven and bake for about 1 hour.

To give your loaf a shiny, professional looking finish, prepare a glaze to brush over the top.

About 5 minutes before the loaf is cooked, measure 1 tablespoon (1 × 15 millilitre spoon) sugar and 2 tablespoons (2 × 15 millilitre spoons) milk into a saucepan.

Heat gently until the sugar dissolves, then bring up to the boil.

Simmer for a moment and draw off the heat.

Remove the baked loaf from the oven, using the oven gloves and turn out of the tin.

Using a pastry brush, brush the loaf all over with the hot glaze to make it shiny.

Leave until cold and then serve sliced with butter and honey.

Makes 1 large loaf

SANDIE BALL
Age 10
Sevenoaks, Kent

Peanut Bars

Ingredients

THE BISCUIT BASE
6 ounces (175 grammes) wholewheat flour
pinch of salt
2 ounces (50 grammes) light soft brown sugar
4 ounces (100 grammes) soft butter

NUT TOPPING
2 egg whites
4 ounces (100 grammes) roasted unsalted peanuts,
    coarsely chopped
4 ounces (100 grammes) light, soft brown sugar

Method

Preheat oven to 350 °F, 180 °C, gas mark 4.

Grease a medium swiss roll tin (13 × 9 inches; 32 × 23 centimetres) with butter.

Sift flour and salt into a bowl. Mix in the sugar and then, using a wooden spoon, mix in the butter to make a smooth dough.

Press this dough into the prepared tin, smooth the top with the back of the spoon.

Bake for 15 minutes.

Meanwhile make the topping: whisk egg whites until stiff and dry and fold in the sugar and chopped nuts.

Remove the tin from the oven and spread the egg whites mixture evenly over the top.

Reduce the oven heat to 300 °F, 150 °C, gas mark 2.

Put back in the oven and bake for another 25 minutes until top is golden brown.

Cut into 24 squares while still warm and leave in the tin to get cold.

NOTE *if only salted peanuts are available, rinse the salt off through a strainer and dry the nuts in the oven for a few minutes.*

Makes 24

ANTHONY DAVIS
Age 10
Slimbridge, Gloucestershire

Main Meals

'Star Wars' Stew

We called it this because it was invented when we wanted a hot meal waiting for us when we came back from seeing the film 'Star Wars'.

Ingredients

fat for frying

1 pound (450 grammes) sausages,
   cut in 1 inch (2 centimetre) slices

2 medium onions (8 ounces; 225 grammes),
   chopped

6 ounces (175 grammes) bacon, chopped

1 small tin (7¾ ounces; 220 grammes) baked beans

1 small tin (7 ounces; 198 grammes) sweetcorn

1 large tin (14 ounces; 397 grammes) tomatoes,
   cut up a bit

1 bayleaf, if you have it

salt and pepper

2 large potatoes (1 pound, 450 grammes) peeled
   and very thinly sliced

TOPPING

1 packet (1½ ounces; 50 grammes) plain crisps,
   crushed
2 ounces (50 grammes) cheese, grated

Method

Heat a little fat in a 5 pint (3 litre) casserole (or if the
casserole is unsuitable for direct heat, brown in a
frying pan and transfer to casserole).

Add sausages, onions, and bacon and brown gently.

Then add the beans, sweetcorn and tomatoes. Add the
bayleaf and season well with salt and pepper.

Top with the thinly sliced potatoes, cover with the lid
or foil and cook gently at 300 °F, 150 °C, gas mark 2, for
about 2½ hours.

Remove the lid and turn heat up to 375 °F, 190 °C, gas
mark 5. Cook for another half hour to slightly brown
the potatoes.

Finally top with crushed crisps and then grated cheese
and put back in the oven until cheese melts.

Serves 4–5

ELSPETH BRUFORD
Age 8
Edinburgh

Eggs Essen

A delicious combination of green pepper, onion, tomatoes, frankfurters and eggs. Eggs Essen is a colourful and substantial meal in itself.

Ingredients

4 tablespoons (4 × 15 millilitre spoons) olive oil
1 medium-sized onion (4 ounces; 100 grammes), finely chopped
2 medium-sized potatoes (about 10 ounces; 275 grammes), peeled and cut into tiny dice
2 ounces (50 grammes) cooked ham, diced
1 small green pepper, white pith removed, seeded and finely chopped
1 small tin (8 ounce; 225 gramme) peeled tomatoes
6–8 frankfurters, cut into ½ inch (1 centimetre) slices
1 teaspoon (1 × 5 millilitre spoon) dried basil
4 eggs
½ teaspoon (½ × 5 millilitre spoon) salt
¼ teaspoon (¼ × 5 millilitre spoon) black pepper

Method

Preheat the oven to very hot: 450 °F, 230 °C, gas mark 8.

In a large frying pan, heat the oil over moderate heat.

Add the onion and potatoes and cook, stirring occasionally, for 5 minutes.

59

Add the ham, green pepper, tomatoes, frankfurters and basil and season with salt and pepper.

Cook, stirring occasionally, for 15 minutes.

Remove the pan from the heat and turn the mixture into a medium-sized shallow oven proof dish.

With a knife, smooth the top of the mixture. Break the eggs on top of the mixture and sprinkle with more salt and pepper.

Place the dish in the upper part of the oven and bake for 10–12 minutes or until the whites of the eggs are set.

Serve at once.

Serves 4

ROSEMARY LARKIN
Age 15
Silsden, West Yorkshire

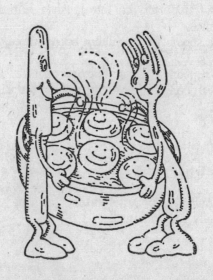

Orkney Bacon Savoury

Ingredients

2 ounces (50 grammes) butter
1 small onion (2 ounces; 50 grammes), chopped
½ pound (225 grammes) bacon, rind removed
    and chopped small
2 eggs, beaten
salt and pepper
6 ounces (175 grammes) grated cheese
4 ounces (100 grammes) fresh white breadcrumbs
3 tomatoes, sliced
¼ pound (100 grammes) mushrooms, chopped

Method

Melt 1 ounce (25 grammes) of the butter in a pan and fry the onion gently for 5 minutes.

Add the bacon and cook for another 5 minutes.

Beat the eggs in a basin and stir in the bacon and onion.

Mix the cheese and breadcrumbs together.

Grease a shallow casserole dish (2 pint; 1.3 litre) and put in layers: half the bacon mixture, half the mushrooms, half the tomatoes, and half the cheese and breadcrumbs mixture.

Repeat the layers once again in the same order, using the remaining ingredients.

Put dabs of the remaining butter on the top and bake for 30 minutes in oven at 400 °F, 200 °C, gas mark 6.

Serves 4

LEONA RENDALL
Age 9
Orkney, Westray

Sausage Lasagne

Ingredients

8 sheets of lasagne, green if possible
1 pound (450 grammes) sausages
1 large tin (14 ounces; 397 grammes) tomatoes
1 ounce (25 grammes) margarine
1 ounce (25 grammes) flour
1 teaspoon (1 × 5 millilitre spoon) mixed herbs
salt and pepper
1 teaspoon (1 × 5 millilitre spoon) worcester
    sauce
2 ounces (50 grammes) cheddar cheese, grated

Method

Grill or fry the sausages, for about 20 minutes.

Meanwhile cook lasagne in plenty of boiling salted
water for 10 minutes, then drain.

Wrap each sausage in a piece of lasagne and put in a shallow dish (2½ pint; 1.3 litre).

Drain tomatoes and make up the juice to ½ pint with water.

Chop the tomatoes and put in with the wrapped sausages.

Melt margarine and add flour, and cook for 2 minutes.

Stir in the juice and bring to the boil.

Simmer until thick. Add the herbs, worcester sauce, salt and pepper and pour over the sausages. Cover with grated cheese.

Cook for about 35 minutes at 375 °F, 190 °C, gas mark 5.

Serves 4

TIMOTHY STYCHE
Age 7
Reading, Berkshire

Cabbage Parcels

Ingredients

1 ounce (25 grammes) dripping
1 small onion (2 ounces; 50 grammes), chopped
½ pound (225 grammes) fresh beef mince
4 ounces (100 grammes) long grain rice
¾ pint (400 millilitres) water
1 beef stock cube
seasoning, salt and pepper
1 large tin (14 ounces; 396 grammes) tomatoes
6 large cabbage leaves

Method

Brown onion in the dripping. Add mince and fry until brown.

Add rice, water, stock cube, seasoning and simmer for 15 minutes until the rice is cooked and all the liquid absorbed.

Cook cabbage leaves in boiling water for 5 minutes, then drain.

Divide the meat mixture between the cabbage leaves and wrap round to make parcels. Put them, rounded side up, in a 2½ pint (1.3 litre) oven-proof dish.

Press the tin of tomatoes through a sieve, season and pour into dish.

Cover and cook in oven for 45 minutes at 350 °F, 180 °C, gas mark 4.

Serves 3

LOUISE COLLINS
Age 13
Carlisle, Cumbria

Orange Chicken with Rosemary

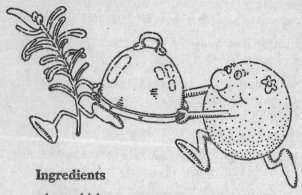

Ingredients

4 large chicken quarters
1 teaspoon (1 × 5 millilitre spoon) salt
½ teaspoon (½ × 5 millilitre spoon) black pepper
3 ounces (75 grammes) butter
2 medium onions (about 8 ounces; 225 grammes)
   thinly sliced
16 fluid ounces (400 millilitres) *unsweetened* fresh
   orange juice
1 tablespoon (1 × 15 millilitre spoon) chopped
   fresh rosemary or 1½ teaspoons (1½ × 5
   millilitre spoon) dried rosemary
2 teaspoons (1 × 5 millilitre spoon) grated orange
   rind
2 tablespoons (2 × 15 millilitre spoon)
   cornflour dissolved in 1 tablespoon (1 × 15
   millilitre spoon) water

Method

Rub the chicken pieces all over with the salt and pepper
and set aside.

In a large oven-proof casserole or saucepan, melt 2 ounces (50 grammes) of the butter over moderate heat.

When the foam subsides, add the chicken pieces and cook, turning occasionally with tongs for 8 to 10 minutes or until they are lightly and evenly browned.

Using tongs remove chicken and set aside. Pour off any remaining browned butter.

Add the remaining 1 ounce (25 grammes) butter to the casserole and when the foam subsides, add the onions and cook, stirring occasionally for 7–10 minutes or until they are soft and translucent, but not brown.

Pour in the orange juice and bring to the boil, stirring occasionally. Stir in the rosemary and orange rind.

Reduce the heat to low and return the chicken pieces to the casserole, or pan. Cover and simmer for about 40 minutes or until the chicken is tender when pierced with the point of a sharp knife.

Using tongs or a slotted spoon, transfer the chicken pieces to a warmed serving dish. Keep warm while you finish the sauce.

Increase the heat to high, and bring the liquid to the boil. Boil for 3 minutes, or until the liquid has reduced slightly. Reduce heat and stir in the cornflour and water mixed. Cook stirring constantly for 2 minutes or until the sauce is hot and thick. Remove from heat and pour over chicken. Serve at once.

Serves 4

PATRICIA O'SULLIVAN
Age 15
London

Chicken Yoghurt

*My recipe is super for a Sunday meal
and it tastes lovely.*

Ingredients

1 × 4 pound (1.8 kilogrammes) chicken, skinned
1 teaspoon (1 × 5 millilitre spoon) salt
juice of ½ lemon
1 teaspoon (1 × 5 millilitre spoon) powdered
    ginger
8 fluid ounces (225 millilitre spoon) natural
    yoghurt
2 garlic cloves, crushed
2 ounces (50 grammes) melted butter

Method

Prick the chicken all over with a fork. Rub the chicken
all over with salt and lemon juice and leave to stand for
about 1 hour.

In a small bowl, combine the yoghurt, ginger and
garlic. Rub this mixture all over the chicken. Cover
and set aside for 3–4 hours.

Preheat the oven to fairly hot: 400 °F, 200 °C, gas mark 6.

Melt the butter in a roasting tin. Put the chicken and
the marinade into the tin and place in the centre of the
oven. Roast for 30 minutes. Reduce the heat to moderate

350 °F, 180 °C, gas mark 4, and continue roasting the chicken, basting frequently with the butter and juices for a further 1–1¼ hours, or until the leg part of the chicken is tender when pierced with the point of a knife.

Remove the roasting tin from the oven. Lift out the chicken and place it on a warmed serving dish.

Place tin over moderate heat and stirring constantly, boil the juices for 3–5 minutes, or until they have thickened.

Pour the sauce over the chicken and serve immediately.

Serve with french beans.

Serves 4

SARAH CHURCHWOOD
Age 13
Bretherton, Lancashire

Guinness Hot Pot

Ingredients

4 tablespoons (4 × 15 millilitre spoons) cooking oil
1 pound (450 grammes) braising steak
½ pint (300 millilitres) can of Guinness
½ pint (300 millilitres) water
½ pound (225 grammes) carrots, sliced
½ pound (225 grammes) onions, chopped
1 level tablespoon (1 × 15 millilitre spoon) flour
1 or 2 cloves of garlic, crushed
salt and black pepper
1 teaspoon (1 × 5 millilitre spoon) white sugar
2 pounds (900 grammes) potatoes

Method

Trim fat off meat and cut into smallish cubes. Brown a few at a time in 2 tablespoons (2 × 15 millilitre spoons) oil over high heat. Keep the browned meat on a plate while the next batch browns.

When all the meat is brown, add the other 2 tablespoons (2 × 15 millilitres) oil to the pan and brown the sliced carrots and chopped onions.

Stir in the flour, sugar and garlic and cook for 1 minute.

Now return the browned meat to the pan. Pour in the Guinness and water and add seasoning.

Put the lid on the pan and simmer gently for $1\frac{1}{2}$ hours until meat and vegetables are tender.

Cook and mash potatoes and add a little milk or cream.

TO SERVE pipe mashed potatoes around edge of the dinner plates serve up meat mixture in the centre.

Serves 4

GWYN JONES
Age 11
Marlborough, Wiltshire

Kipper and Egg Flan

Ingredients

FOR THE PASTRY
4 ounces (100 grammes) plain flour
pinch of salt
2 ounces (50 grammes) margarine
2 ounces (50 grammes) grated cheese
2 tablespoons (2 × 15 millilitre spoons) water

FOR THE FILLING
7 ounce (200 gramme) packet boneless kipper
   fillets
4 eggs, separated
3 ounces (75 grammes) grated cheese
salt and pepper
small green pepper, cut into rings

Method

Heat the oven to 400 °F, 200 °C, gas mark 6.

Sift the flour and salt into a bowl.

Add margarine and rub in until mixture resembles fine
bread crumbs.

Add cheese and mix well.

Mix to a stiff consistency with water. Roll out on
floured board.

Line an 8 inch (20 centimetre) flan tin. Bake the flan case for about 20 minutes. Reduce oven heat to 350 °F, 180 °C, gas mark 4.

Drain the kippers and flake coarsely. Arrange over base of flan case.

Separate eggs and beat yolks until smooth. Add half the cheese and pour over kippers. Season.

Whisk whites until stiff, fold in remaining cheese, salt and pepper and pile on top of flan. Bake in centre of oven for 20–25 minutes until golden brown.

Garnish with green pepper rings. Serve hot or cold.

Serves 6

MARK TREE
Age 12
Ipswich, Suffolk

Hot and Cold Puddings

Granny's Lemon Pudding

Ingredients

2 ounces (50 grammes) self-raising flour
3 ounces (75 grammes) margarine
5 ounces (125 grammes) caster sugar
3 eggs – separated
½ pint (300 millilitres) milk
rind and juice of 1 lemon

Method

Preheat oven to 350 °F, 180 °C, gas mark 4.

Cream the fat and sugar together.

Add yolks, rind, juice and flour.

Mix well and add milk slowly till mixture becomes a thick batter.

Whisk egg whites stiffly and fold until mixture.

Pour into a greased 2–2½ pint (1.3 litre) dish and stand the dish in a tin of cold water.

Place in oven and cook for ¼ hour at 350 °F, 180 °C, gas mark 4.

Reduce to 325 °F, 170 °C, gas mark 3, for about another ½ hour until golden brown on top.

Decorate with a slice of lemon if liked and serve hot or cold.

RESULT *lemony sponge at the top and a lovely lemony sauce at the bottom.*

Serves 4–6

DEBORAH JONES
Age 14
Lichfield, Staffs

No-Bake Banana Cheesecake

Ingredients

BASE

4 ounces (100 grammes) crushed digestive
    biscuits
2 ounces (50 grammes) melted butter
1 ounce (25 grammes) caster sugar

TOPPING

5 fluid ounces (150 millilitres) double cream
3 ounces (75 grammes) Philadelphia cream cheese
1 tablespoon (1 × 15 millilitre spoon) lemon
    juice
1 ounce (25 grammes) caster sugar
3 firm bananas
1 ounce (25 grammes) browned flaked almonds
    to decorate

Method

Crush biscuits with a rolling pin and mix with butter and sugar.

Press into an 8 inch (20 centimetre) sponge tin or flan dish.

Put in the fridge for ½ –1 hour.

Beat lemon juice into the cheese and gradually beat in the cream until smooth.

Add sugar and fold in sliced bananas.

Spoon over the biscuit base and sprinkle with almonds.

Serves 6

SOFIA HOGGART
Age 12
Northfleet, Kent

Butterscotch Bananas

Ingredients

4 bananas
3 ounces (75 grammes) soft brown sugar
1 ounce (25 grammes) butter
2 tablespoons (2 × 15 millilitre spoons) lemon
    juice
2 tablespoons (2 × 15 millilitre spoons) water

Method

Before you begin, turn on the grill – not too high.

Peel bananas and cut them in half lengthways and
sprinkle with lemon juice. Put them in an oven-proof
baking dish and set it aside.

Put the sugar, butter and water into a small saucepan.

Place over *low* heat and cook gently until the butter has
melted and the sugar dissolved, stirring with a wooden
spoon. The mixture will thicken a bit.

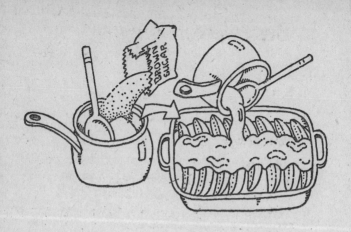

Remove from heat and pour the sauce over the bananas.

Put the dish under the grill and grill for 5 minutes, until the mixture is bubbly.

Remove from grill and eat at once (they are lovely hot with ice cream) or leave to cool.

Serves 4

JOANNE COWLEY
Age 8
Manchester

Cranachan

Ingredients

2 ounces (50 grammes) medium or coarse oatmeal
½ pint (300 millilitres) double (heavy) cream
¼ pint (125 millilitres) single (light) cream
caster sugar to taste
few drops of vanilla essence or
    2–3 tablespoons (2–3 × 15 millilitre spoons)
    of any liquor or rum
10 ounces (275 grammes) fresh raspberries,
    strawberries etc.

Method

Toast the oatmeal until lightly brown, either under a grill, in the oven or in a frying pan. Cool.

Whisk the creams together until thick, but not stiff and add the sugar and essence to taste.

Fold in oatmeal, followed by the fresh fruit, keeping 6 berries for decorating.

Spoon into 6 individual dishes and top with the reserved fruit.

Serve chilled soon after making.

NOTE *if the coarse grade of oatmeal is used it toasts better and increases the nutty taste. Do not try to use rolled oats otherwise the Cranachan goes stodgy. Strawberries should be halved or sliced before adding to the cream.*

Serves 6

KIRSTY STEWARDSON
Age 11
Aberfeldy, Perthshire

Apple and Honey Dessert

Ingredients

1 large cooking apple (12 ounces; 350 grammes),
   peeled, cored and chopped
4 ounces (100 grammes) self-raising flour
3 ounces (75 grammes) suet
2 ounces (50 grammes) fresh breadcrumbs
3 tablespoons (3 × 15 millilitre spoons) honey
¼ pint (150 millilitres) milk
1 tablespoon (1 × 15 millilitre spoon) caster
   sugar to sprinkle on top

Method

Mix all the ingredients together in a basin.

Spoon into a greased 1½ pint (1 litre) oven proof dish.

Bake for about 40 minutes at 350 °F, 180 °C, gas mark 4,
until golden brown.

Sprinkle the top with castor sugar.

Eat it hot and it is really nice.

Serves 4

JUSTINE
FRECKNALL
Age 5
Horley, Surrey

84

Bramble Bombe

Ingredients

PURÉE

1 pound (450 grammes) blackberries (fresh or
   frozen)
4 ounces (100 grammes) sugar

Method

Place blackberries and sugar in a saucepan. Cover and
cook gently until the fruit is soft.

Cool slightly and rub the fruit through a sieve.

Makes approximately 1 pint (575 millilitres).

CREAM MIXTURE

¼ pint (150 millilitres) double cream
¼ pint (150 millilitres) single cream
2 handfuls (about 2 ounces; 50 grammes) of
   broken meringues
¼ pint (150 millilitres) double cream for
   decorating.

Method

Measure ½ pint (285 millilitres) of the purée (keep the
rest for the sauce).

Whip the creams together until fluffy and fold in the
meringue pieces.

Carefully add the purée, folding into the cream and
meringue mixture. Be careful not to overfold – it
should have a marbled effect.

Put into a 2 pint (1.3 litre) basin and freeze *or* put into
some prewashed margarine containers (those with lids)
and freeze. These are just right for individual servings.

When ready to serve, dip basin or margarine tubs into handhot water and turn on to a plate. Spoon a little of the reserved purée over the top and serve the rest separately.
(If a softer texture bombe is required, take out of the freezer and put into the fridge for 1 hour before serving.)

TO DECORATE
whip the remaining $\frac{1}{4}$ pint (150 millilitres) double cream to dab on the top. Angelica, glacé cherries or a few whole blackberries can also be added for effect.

This can also be made with other soft fruits.

Serves 6–8

ERICA WATSON
Age 15
Weymouth, Dorset

Sweets and drinks

Honey Health Candy

Here is my favourite recipe. It is very yummy. It would be good for Simon and Chris to get more energy when they do their daring things. Also, it will not rot your teeth.

Ingredients

4 ounces (100 grammes) chopped dried apricots
4 fluid ounces (100 millilitres) water
2 ounces (50 grammes) finely chopped almonds
1 tablespoon (1 × 15 millilitre spoon) lemon juice
1 teaspoon (1 × 5 millilitre spoon) lemon rind
3–4 tablespoons (3–4 × 15 millilitre spoons) honey
2 ounces (50 grammes) skim milk powder
1 tablespoon (1 × 15 millilitre spoon) wheatgerm – optional
3 ounces (75 grammes) sultanas
2 ounces (50 grammes) dessicated coconut

1 ounce (25 grammes) extra dessicated coconut

Method

Combine the apricots and water in a saucepan. Bring to the boil, reduce the heat and simmer until just tender and water is absorbed – 3–4 minutes.

Remove from heat, combine apricot mixture with almonds, lemon juice, lemon rind, skim milk powder, wheatgerm, if used, sultanas and coconut.

Mix to a firm paste with the honey.

Divide the mixture into three; wet hands and form mixture into rolls, about 8 inches (20.5 centimetres) long. Roll in extra coconut.

Rolls can be cut into slices and eaten after being refrigerated for several hours. They taste even better if kept in the refrigerator over night – the flavours have time to blend and mature.

Makes about $1\frac{1}{4}$ pounds (550 grammes)

SANDALIN BOAG
Age 8
Fife, St Andrews

Grandma's Stick Jaw Toffee

Ingredients

6 ounces (175 grammes) butter
1 small (7 ounce; 200 gramme) tin condensed
  milk
8 ounces (225 grammes) soft brown sugar
8 ounces (225 grammes) golden syrup

Method

Melt the butter in a large saucepan.

Add the sugar and syrup and heat gently to dissolve the sugar.

Stir until it boils and add condensed milk.

Boil steadily for about 20 minutes, stirring all the time with a wooden spoon. It will thicken and go a medium 'oak' colour.

TO TEST FOR READINESS
Drop small amount into a saucer of cold water. It should form a soft, round ball.

Pour quickly into a greased tin (11 × 7 inches; 28 × 18 centimetres).

Leave to set and get cold. Then break into pieces and store in a tin.

Make with mum's help as the mixture gets hot. Don't forget to clean your teeth after eating it!

Makes about 1¾ pounds (675 grammes)

NICHOLAS JON WARD
Age 8
Morpeth, Northumberland

Mocha Fudge

Ingredients

3 ounces (75 grammes) Philadelphia cream cheese
12 ounces (350 grammes) icing sugar (sieved)
3 teaspoons (3 × 5 millilitre spoons) instant
    coffee dissolved in 2 teaspoons (2 × 5
    millilitre spoons) of boiling water
2 ounces (50 grammes) plain chocolate
2 ounces (50 grammes) raisins

Method

Beat the cheese until soft and smooth.

Gradually add the icing sugar and beat well to avoid lumps.

Melt the chocolate in a basin over a saucepan of hot water, then let it cool a little.

Beat the coffee, chocolate and the raisins into the cheese mixture.

Put into a tin, roughly 6 × 6 inches (15 × 15 centimetres), lined with greaseproof paper, and press smooth.

Leave in the refrigerator for about 1 hour or leave overnight if a firmer fudge is preferred.

Cut into 1 inch (2½ centimetre) squares when set.

If desired, place a walnut half on each square.

Makes 1¼ pounds (550 grammes)

ANNA-MARIE BASSETT
Age 15
Stourbridge, West Midlands

Orange Cocktail

Ingredients

¼ pint (150 millilitres) strained fresh orange juice
2 tablespoons (2 × 15 millilitre spoons) lemon
    juice
1 tablespoon (1 × 15 millilitre spoon) caster
    sugar
¼ pint (150 millilitres) ginger ale or soda water
3 glacé, or cocktail, cherries
3 cocktail sticks

Method

Mix the fruit juice
and the sugar, and
allow it to dissolve.
Just before serving,
add the ginger ale,
pour into small
cocktail glasses and
garnish with a little
cherry on a stick.

Serve very cold.

Serves 3

Anita Jane Tomlinson
Age 11
Blackpool, Lancashire

Strawberry Marshmallow Float Drink

Ingredients

2 cartons (5 fluid ounces)
  strawberry yoghurt
1 pint (575 millilitres)
  cold milk
caster sugar, if liked
8 marshmallows

Method

Whisk milk and yoghurt together until frothy, and add a little sugar to taste.

Pour into glasses.

Float marshmallows on the top.

Chill and serve with two straws.

Serves 4

LINDA GOODWIN
Age 12
Rishton, Lancashire